OPTIMISTIC MEMORY

LEARN FASTER AND REMEMBER MORE

ABHIT TOMAR

Made with ♥ on the Notion Press Platform
www.notionpress.com

To my family,
for your unwavering love, support, and belief in me.

To my friends,
who stood by me through every step of this journey,
offering encouragement, laughter, and inspiration.

And to everyone who has ever doubted their ability to learn—
this book is for you. May it help you unlock the true potential of your mind.

Contents

Foreword

Welcome to this journey of enhancing your memory and improving your learning techniques. My name is **AbhitTomar**, and like many of you, I've been through the grind of competitive exam preparation, specifically the UPSC Civil Services Exam (CSE). When I first began my journey, memory was a constant challenge. I felt overwhelmed by the sheer volume of information I needed to remember—notes, books, dates, and countless facts.

But as I dove deeper into my psychology optional subject, I learned that memory isn't something you're born with or without. It's a skill. And like any skill, it can be developed, sharpened, and mastered.

This book is for anyone who has ever felt that their memory isn't up to the task. Whether you're a student preparing for exams or someone who simply wants to improve their memory for daily tasks, I've compiled everything I've learned—from the science behind memory to practical tips and exercises you can start using right away.

It's important to know that I wasn't always someone with a strong memory. In fact, I had trouble remembering my own study schedule, let alone the intricate details of subjects like Indian polity or history. But with a little persistence, and by using the techniques shared in this book, I transformed my approach to learning. This is the same path I'll guide you through.

By the end of this book, you'll have the tools, insights, and practical exercises to train your memory, focus better, and bring life to the information you study. Memory isn't about memorization; it's about understanding, linking ideas, and applying what you've learned. So, let's get started and unlock the full potential of your brain!

Introduction

Memory is one of our most powerful tools, yet it's often misunderstood and underutilized. For anyone preparing for exams, like the UPSC Civil Services Exam (CSE), SSC, GATE, NET, or simply looking to improve their ability to retain and recall information, memory is the key to success. But memory isn't just about cramming facts and figures into your brain—it's about understanding how to make information stick, how to retrieve it when you need it, and how to keep your brain sharp in the long run.

This book guides anyone who feels overwhelmed by the vast amount of information they need to absorb. It's for the students who spend hours studying but still struggle to recall key facts during an exam. It's for the professionals who want to enhance their memory for everyday tasks. And it's for the lifelong learners who want to unlock the full potential of their brain.

As someone who prepared for the UPSC CSE, I've been where you are. I've experienced the frustration of reading and re-reading notes, only to forget them a few days later. But through research, practice, and trial and error, I discovered that memory is a skill—a skill that can be trained, honed, and improved. In fact, anyone can improve their memory, regardless of where they start.

This book combines both the science of memory and practical, easy-to-apply techniques. From understanding the basics of how memory works to mastering advanced strategies like the memory palace and pegging technique, you'll find tools to help you retain information more effectively. We'll also explore creative techniques—like visualization, storytelling, and turning numbers into images—that will make studying more enjoyable and productive.

The goal of this book is simple: to help you learn smarter, not harder. Whether you're preparing for one of India's toughest exams or just trying to remember people's names more easily, the strategies here will change the way you approach learning and memory. You'll find exercises, personal anecdotes, and science-backed tips that are designed to fit seamlessly into your study routine.

By the end of this book, you'll have a deeper understanding of how memory works and a powerful set of tools to help you boost your retention and recall. The techniques are flexible—you can adapt them to your learning style and the kind of material you're working with. Above all, this book will help you develop a mindset that sees memory not as a challenge, but as an exciting part of the learning process.

Let's get started on unlocking the full potential of your memory.

Abhit Tomar

ONE

The Science of Memory: Why It Matters

> "The true art of memory is the art of attention."
> -**Samuel Johnson**

Imagine sitting down with a pile of books in front of you, ready to study, but feeling like no matter how much you read, nothing sticks. This was me during my UPSC prep days. The constant frustration of reading and forgetting haunted me until I started digging into the psychology of memory. Understanding how memory works was the game changer.

What Is Memory, Really?

Memory is your brain's ability to store, retain, and recall information. In simple terms, it's how we remember things—from something as simple as your phone number to complex ideas like constitutional amendments or syntax of java or python programming language. Memory isn't just a vault where we stuff facts; it's a dynamic process that involves three stages:

1. **Encoding**: This is when you first encounter information, like reading a history chapter or listening to a lecture. Your brain converts the information into a form that it can store.
2. **Storage**: Once encoded, this information gets stored in your brain, either in short-term memory (where it might last a few minutes) or

long-term memory (where it can last years).

3. **Retrieval**: This is where the magic happens—when you're able to recall information when you need it, like during an exam or even in a casual conversation or during interview.

It sounds simple, but the way these three processes work can be affected by many factors—stress, sleep, attention, and even how we approach learning in the first place.

Why Memory Matters for Learning

Memory plays a massive role in everything you do, especially in learning. Let's take the UPSC exam or any other competitive exam as an example. You're expected to retain an enormous amount of information, and without a good memory, it can feel like trying to fill a bucket with water while there's a hole in the bottom.

But here's something you might not know: **memory is more about understanding and organizing than pure repetition**. When you truly understand a concept, your brain creates stronger connections between related ideas, making it easier to store and recall that information later.

Think of it like this—your brain is a vast network, and the more you understand a concept, the stronger the pathways are between different pieces of information. These pathways make it easier for you to retrieve information when you need it. This is why rote memorization (simply repeating something over and over) often fails in the long term. It doesn't create meaningful connections.

The Science Behind It

Let's get a bit scientific for a moment. The brain stores memories in different regions. One crucial area is the **hippocampus**, which is like the brain's librarian—it helps categorize and store your memories. When you learn something new, neurons (the cells in your brain) fire together and create connections. The more you revisit that information, the stronger these connections become.

> “*"The brain is the most adaptive organ in the body. It can change and rewire itself throughout your entire life"* - ***Dr Andrew Huberman***”

Ever wondered why you can recall childhood memories so vividly, yet struggle to remember what you studied last week? That's because **long-term memories are formed through repetition and emotional significance.**

When something has emotional value or is tied to a strong experience, it gets stamped in your brain more permanently.

Practical Tips to Enhance Memory

Let me break down some simple strategies that helped me improve my memory, especially during my UPSC preparation:

1. **Understand First, Memorize Later**: The biggest mistake is trying to memorize something you don't fully understand. Take time to break down the material into simpler parts. Ask yourself: Do I really know what this concept means?
2. **Use Visuals**: Our brain is great at remembering pictures and visuals. So, when you study, try drawing diagrams or mind maps. This is particularly useful in subjects like geography or science or if you are software developer then visuals really help to solve problems.
3. **Teach What You Learn**: One of the best ways to strengthen your memory is by teaching what you've learned to someone else. When you teach, you're forced to organize the information in your head clearly.
4. **Take Breaks**: Our brain needs rest. Studying for long hours without a break can actually hurt your memory. The **Pomodoro technique** (studying for 25 minutes and then taking a 5-minute break) can help keep your brain fresh.

Why This Book Matters

At the end of the day, memory isn't just about cramming facts for an exam. It's about creating a solid foundation that you can build upon. Memory allows you to not just pass exams but to truly master the subjects you're studying.

In the chapters that follow, we're going to explore practical techniques and strategies to improve your memory. Some will be based on science, others on my personal experiences from UPSC preparation and IT interview prep, but all of them are designed to help you retain information better and boost your overall learning.

So, are you ready to dive deeper into the world of memory? Trust me, it's not as complicated as it sounds—just a few tweaks to your approach can make all the difference.

TWO

FOCUS: THE FIRST STEP TO LEARNING

"*"The successful warrior is the average man, with laser-like focus."*
Bruce Lee"

If memory is the foundation of learning, then focus is the hammer that shapes it. You might have noticed that no matter how many hours you spend staring at a book, nothing sticks if your mind is drifting. That was me during the early days of my UPSC preparation. I would sit down to study, but within minutes, I'd get distracted. It wasn't until I learned how to focus properly that my memory and learning took a sharp turn for the better.

The Problem with Distractions

Distractions are everywhere—phones buzzing with notifications, thoughts wandering off, or simply the stress of thinking about how much you have to cover, what will be future or getting 12LPA in 1st corporate interview. In today's world, we are surrounded by distractions that pull us in every direction. But here's the good news: focusing is a skill, just like memory, and it can be improved with practice.

The key is to understand that **our brain needs to be in the present moment to absorb information effectively**. When you're fully engaged with what you're studying, your brain encodes that information more efficiently. This brings us to the first principle of focus:

Mindfulness: Being Present in the Moment

You've probably heard of mindfulness in Sadhguru YouTube videos or somewhere else, but what does it have to do with memory and learning?

Well, mindfulness is all about being aware of the present moment—what you're doing, what you're feeling, and where your thoughts are. The more mindful you are while studying, the better your brain will be at remembering what you're learning.

In my own experience, I found that when I was mentally scattered—thinking about my next meal, worrying about my study schedule, working on Plan B i.e Software engineer or wondering how I would ever finish the syllabus—I retained almost nothing. My mind was everywhere except on my books.

> "*"It is not enough to be busy... The question is: What are we busy about?" — **Henry David Thoreau***"

Once I started practicing mindfulness, though, my focus sharpened. It didn't happen overnight, but little by little, I trained my mind to stay in the moment. Here's how you can do it:

Practical Focus Exercises

1. **The Two-Minute Mindful Focus Exercise**:
    - Before you start studying, take two minutes to sit quietly. Close your eyes and focus on your breathing. Breathe in slowly, hold it for a second, then breathe out. As you do this, notice how your body feels—how your mind is clearing. This simple exercise helps **reset** your brain and prepares it to focus on the task at hand.
2. **The Pomodoro Technique**:
    - One of the simplest and most effective methods to improve focus is the Pomodoro technique. Here's how it works: Set a timer for 25 minutes and focus entirely on your work during that time. Switch off your mobile. Once the timer goes off, take a 5-minute break. After four Pomodoro (25-minute sessions), take a longer break (15–30 minutes). This method works wonders because it trains your brain to concentrate in short bursts, making study sessions more effective.
3. **One-Task-At-A-Time Rule**:

- Multitasking is a myth. Studies show that when we try to juggle multiple tasks, our brain becomes less efficient. The same goes for studying. *Focus on one subject, one task, and one page at a time* Just like *One Nation, One Election*. When I was preparing for my exams, I used to jump from one book to another, thinking I was saving time. But I was making it harder for my brain to retain anything. Once I started giving my full attention to one topic, I noticed a huge improvement in both my focus and memory.

Personal Example: My Focus Struggles

Let me share a little about my journey with focus. In the early stages of my UPSC preparation, I used to sit with all my study materials spread out, thinking I could cover multiple subjects at once. Making To-Do list extensive with covering 3-4 subjects in one day with multiple chapter. I'd read a few pages of history, then switch to geography, then flip through some notes on economics. It felt like I was doing a lot, but at the end of the day, I remembered almost nothing.

I realized I was spending more time getting distracted than actually studying. So I made a change. I started practicing mindfulness and using the Pomodoro technique. Instead of bouncing between topics, I dedicated a solid 25 minutes to just one subject. Then I'd take a break and switch to the next. This simple shift made a massive difference in my focus, and as a result, my retention improved significantly.

Tips to Improve Focus While Studying

1. **Create a Distraction-Free Study Zone**:

    - This is one of the simplest but most effective ways to improve focus. Find a quiet place to study. Aspirants in Delhi used to go to study room (Library). Clear your desk of anything unrelated to your work. Put your phone in another room or Bag if possible, or use apps that block distracting notifications during study time. I used to leave my phone in my room and visit the library during my UPSC prep and interview prep for the company, and trust me, it helped me focus like nothing else.

2. **Set Specific Goals**:

- Every study session should have a clear, specific objective. Instead of a vague goal like "studying history," break it into smaller tasks, such as "I'll read and summarize the Mughal Empire's administration in 25 minutes." Similarly, instead of saying "I'll complete Java and Data Structures today," focus on specific topics like "Java strings" or "bubble sort in DSA."

Setting clear, manageable goals helps you stay focused and gives your brain a sense of accomplishment when you complete each task, boosting motivation and productivity.

3. **Take Regular Breaks**:

   - Studying for hours on end without a break will only make your brain sluggish. Breaks are necessary to keep your mind sharp. Use the Pomodoro technique to structure your breaks, or simply stand up and stretch for a couple of minutes after every 30–45 minutes of study. When you return, your mind will be refreshed, and you'll be able to focus better.

> *"If you want to learn anything faster, the key is to focus on something intensely for short periods, then give your brain some space to rest and consolidate the information."*

Why Focus and Memory Go Hand in Hand

Here's the thing: If you're not focused, you can't form strong memories. Think of focus as the spotlight on a stage, and your brain as the actor trying to perform. Without that spotlight, the actor gets lost in the dark, and no one remembers the performance. Similarly, without focus, your brain can't properly encode the information you're trying to learn.

Once you train your brain to focus, your memory automatically improves because the information you study is getting the attention it needs to stick. You can think of it like building a focus is the foundation, and memory is the structure that stands on top of it. Without a solid foundation, the whole structure collapses.

Thoughts on Focus

Learning how to focus doesn't just help with studying for exams—it's a life skill that will benefit you in everything you do. The more you practice mindfulness, eliminate distractions, and commit to one task at a time, the better your brain will get at encoding and recalling information. And trust me, once you master this, your learning will skyrocket.

So, take a deep breath, focus on the present, and let's continue this journey of enhancing your memory!

THREE

BUSTING COMMON MEMORY MYTHS

"*"What we think, we become."* - ***Buddha***"

When it comes to memory, we've all heard things like, "I'm just not good at remembering things," or "Some people have natural photographic memory." These are common beliefs that, for many of us, end up limiting our potential. But here's the truth: **memory is a skill, not a talent you're born with**. Just like learning to ride a bike or play a musical instrument, anyone can improve their memory with the right techniques and a little practice.

As someone who started with what I believed was a "weak memory" during my UPSC prep, I can assure you that it's not about how much you can memorize—it's about how you approach learning and retention. Let's break down some of the biggest myths about memory and uncover the real facts.

Myth #1: "I Have a Bad Memory"

This is probably the most common myth I hear, and I used to believe it myself. But here's the reality: most people don't have a bad memory, they just haven't learned the right techniques to enhance it. Memory isn't something that you're stuck with, like a fixed IQ. Your brain is **plastic**, meaning it's constantly changing and adapting. This concept is known as **neuroplasticity** (you may have heard it in Dr. Andrew Huberman's interview on YouTube), and it means that with practice, you can train your brain to retain more information.

Fact: Memory is like a muscle—the more you use it, the stronger it gets.

Think of your brain as a set of muscles. When you don't train it, it becomes weak and sluggish. But when you actively engage it—by challenging yourself to remember new things, using techniques like visualization, or even playing memory games—it gets stronger.

Myth #2: "Some People Are Born with a Photographic Memory"

We all know someone who seems to remember everything with ease as if their brain takes mental snapshots of everything they see. This leads to the belief that these people are somehow born with a **photographic memory**, which allows them to perfectly recall every detail of what they see or read. One of my friends, Neeraj Kumar (PhD, IIIT Delhi), has a photographic memory. He can remember dates, names, events, and locations simply by listening, reading, or visiting. However, science suggests that **true photographic memory is incredibly rare**, and most people who seem to have exceptional memories have simply learned techniques that help them recall information more effectively.

Fact: Exceptional memory is often the result of using specific techniques, not natural talent.

Most people with great memories use methods like **mnemonics, chunking**, or **visualization** to help them store and recall information. They don't rely on some magical ability to remember everything—they've just trained their brain to use these strategies effectively.

During my studies, I often met people who seemed to remember pages of books without breaking a sweat. I later discovered that they were using methods like the **memory palace technique**, where you imagine placing information in specific locations in your mind or creating mental images to represent facts. Once I started using these techniques, I found that my recall improved dramatically, even though I never thought I could have that kind of memory.

Myth #3: "Rote Memorization Is the Best Way to Remember"

Many students believe that repeating information over and over is the best way to remember things. This is called **rote memorization**—where you drill facts into your brain by sheer repetition. But here's the thing: while rote learning can help with short-term recall, it doesn't necessarily help with **long-term memory retention**. Simply memorizing facts without understanding them can often lead to forgetting the information soon after you've learned it. You can try to remember the title and quotes of chapter 1 of this book

Fact: Understanding and connecting ideas is far more effective than pure repetition.

Memory works best when you're able to **understand** the information and make connections between ideas. This is because when you truly grasp a concept, your brain creates a **network of associations** around it, making it easier to recall later. Instead of focusing on repetition, try to break down the material, relate it to what you already know, and make meaningful connections.

> *"Neuroplasticity allows your brain to change with experience—memory is not fixed"*

Example:
Let's say you're trying to remember historical events for an exam. Instead of repeating the dates and events over and over, try understanding the context of each event. Why did it happen? What were the consequences? How does it relate to other events? By creating these connections, your brain will naturally retain the information better.

Myth #4: "Memory Declines with Age"

It's a common belief that as we get older, our memory naturally starts to fade. While it's true that certain cognitive functions can slow down with age, the idea that memory inevitably declines is misleading. Studies show that **older adults can improve their memory just like younger people** through mental exercises and techniques.

Fact: Memory can be maintained and even improved with age.

The key to maintaining a strong memory is **continuous mental engagement**. Just like your body, your brain needs regular exercise to stay fit. This could be through learning new skills, reading, solving puzzles, or even practicing memory techniques. It's never too late to start working on your memory.
Research has shown that older adults who engage in activities like learning a new language or practicing creative hobbies maintain better cognitive function than those who don't challenge their brains.

Myth #5: "The More You Study, the More You'll Remember"

This is another common myth that many students fall into, especially during exam season. Reading 13-16hr in day can ace exams is a common myth among students. We often think that the more hours we spend studying, the more we'll remember. But in reality, **quality trumps quantity** when it comes to studying. Spending long hours cramming information into your brain without proper breaks can harm your memory.

Fact: It's not about how long you study, but how effectively you study.

Studying for long periods without breaks can cause **mental fatigue**, leading to decreased focus and poor retention. Instead, try using **spaced repetition**—where you break your study sessions into short, focused chunks with regular breaks. This method allows your brain to process the information more effectively and helps with long-term retention.

Personal Experience:

During my preparation, I used to spend hours studying non-stop in the Library, thinking I was being productive. However, I often found myself forgetting most of what I had studied. It wasn't until I started using techniques like the **Pomodoro method** (25 minutes of focused study followed by a 5-minute short break) and spaced repetition that I noticed a significant improvement in my memory.

The key takeaway from busting these myths is simple: **your memory is not fixed**. It's a skill that can be improved with the right techniques, mindset, and practice. Whether you're studying for an exam or just trying to improve your memory for everyday tasks, knowing the truth about how memory works can help you unlock its full potential.

FOUR

VISUALIZATION: MAKE INFORMATION STICK

> "“*Visualize this thing that you want, see it, feel it, believe in it. Make your mental blueprint and begin to build.*”- ***Robert Collier***"

Have you ever tried to memorize something, only to forget it almost instantly? I certainly have. But what if I told you there's a technique that makes it easier to remember even the most complex concepts? That technique is **visualization.**

Visualization is all about creating mental images that bring the information you're learning to life. Our brain is naturally wired to remember images better than abstract words or numbers. Think about it: you're more likely to remember a vivid scene from a movie than a list of dry facts from a textbook, right? That's because our brain has evolved to process and store visual information more effectively. So, why not use this to your advantage while studying or working in office?

Why Visualization Works

The science behind visualization is fascinating. When you create mental images, you're engaging multiple parts of your brain, including those responsible for vision, memory, and emotions (The **occipital lobe** processes vision, the **hippocampus** regulates memory, and the **amygdala** governs emotions.). This helps create stronger neural connections, which makes it easier to recall the information later. In fact, studies show that **visualizing concepts makes them up to 65% more memorable** compared to simply reading or listening.

Here's why this technique works:

- **Engages Multiple Senses**: Visualization taps into both your visual and cognitive memory, making the information more engaging.
- **Strengthens Memory Pathways**: By turning abstract information into concrete images, your brain creates stronger connections that are easier to recall.
- **Increases Emotional Engagement**: When you create vivid images, your brain also associates emotions with the material, which makes it more likely to stick.

How to Use Visualization for Studying

1. **Turn Facts into Pictures** One of the simplest ways to use visualization is to turn abstract facts into concrete images. For example, if you're studying geography and trying to remember the location of mountain ranges, imagine the mountains rising up in your mind's eye. Picture the Himalayas towering above, snow-capped and majestic, instead of just memorizing that "the Himalayas are in Northern India."

Example:

When I was studying history , I struggled with remembering the dates and key events of the Mughal Empire. So instead of trying to memorize facts, I imagined a grand timeline stretching out before me. On one side, I saw Babur with his army entering India, and further along, I pictured Akbar in his court with advisors and ministers. Similarly, in web development, when we visualize the structure of a website or a database, we can better recall the correct functions and syntax, making them stick longer in our memory. Creating these mental images has also helped me remember events more easily when I need to.

Use Mind Maps

Another powerful visualization tool is the **mind map**. Mind maps are diagrams that help you organize information visually. They're great for breaking down complex topics into bite-sized, manageable parts, and they allow you to see the relationships between different concepts.

How to Create a Mind Map:

- Start with a central idea or topic (for example, "Indian Polity").

- Branch out with subtopics like "Constitution," "Legislature," and "Judiciary."
- Add smaller branches for more specific details (like "Article 370" under "Constitution" or "Rajya Sabha" under "Legislature").

Mind maps allow you to visualize how ideas connect, making it easier for your brain to store and retrieve the information.

1. **Storytelling as a Visualization Tool**
   We humans have been telling stories for thousands of years, and there's a reason why stories are so memorable. When you turn information into a story, it gives context and meaning to the facts, making them easier to remember. You can use storytelling to visualize historical events, scientific processes, or even mathematical formulas.

Let's say you're trying to remember the steps of a biological process, like photosynthesis. Instead of just memorizing the steps, imagine the story of a leaf waking up in the morning, soaking up sunlight, and converting it into food. Visualize the chloroplasts inside the leaf as tiny factories, working hard to produce energy. This mental image, wrapped in a story, will make the process much easier to remember.

3. **Link Abstract Ideas with Familiar Images**
   One of the best ways to make difficult or abstract concepts memorable is to link them with familiar images. This technique is often used in the **memory palace** method, where you imagine placing items or information in specific locations in a familiar space (like your home or school). When you need to recall the information, you mentally walk through that space and pick up the information you've stored there.

If you're trying to remember different types of taxes (like direct and indirect taxes), imagine walking into your living room and seeing a large stack of money on your couch (representing direct taxes like income tax). In the kitchen, you see a bunch of products lined up, each with a price tag like Tata Tea, Cashew, Biscuits, Bread, etc (representing indirect taxes like GST). By linking the abstract idea of taxation to familiar objects in your house, your brain will find it much easier to recall later.

Exercise: Try Visualization Now

Let's put this into practice. Pick something you're studying right now and try visualizing it. Here's a step-by-step guide to help you get started:

1. **Close your eyes and imagine** the concept you're trying to learn as clearly as possible. If it's a historical event, picture the people involved, the environment, and what's happening around them. If it's a scientific concept, imagine the process step by step.
2. **Add details** to make the image more vivid. What colors, shapes, or emotions do you associate with this image? The more detail you add, the more likely you'll remember it.

"*Make your task attractive, and your brain will naturally follow.*"

3. **Connect the visual image** to something you already know. For example, if you're visualizing a chemical reaction, link it to a process you've seen before, like baking a cake or watching ice melt.
4. **Revisit the image regularly**. The more you visualize, the stronger the connection will be in your brain. This is a technique that improves with practice.

Personal Experience: How Visualization Helped Me in UPSC

During my preparation, one of the most difficult subjects for me was Indian geography in remembering facts. There were so many rivers, mountain ranges, and cities to remember, and I couldn't keep track of them all. That's when I started using visualization.

Instead of staring at maps and lists of names, I imagined myself flying over India. I had start in the north, flying over the Himalayas, picturing the rivers like the Indus, Ganga and Yamuna snaking their way down and their tributaries. As I flew south, I'd pass over the plains, into the Western Ghats, and down to the tip of Tamil Nadu.

This mental journey helped me not only remember the locations of geographical features but also gave me a deeper understanding of how they're connected. And during the exam, it was like I was taking that flight again, recalling the places with ease.

Final views on Visualization

Visualization is one of the most powerful tools for improving memory, and the best part is, you can use it for almost anything you're learning. Whether it's turning boring facts into lively images or creating mind maps to organize your thoughts, visualization makes learning more engaging, more memorable.

FIVE

MEMORY AIDS YOU CAN USE RIGHT NOW

"Small disciplines repeated with consistency every day lead to great achievements gained slowly over time."

- **John C. Maxwell**

When most people think of memory techniques, they imagine complex systems that require a lot of time and effort. But in reality, some of the best memory aids are all around us—in the objects we use every day and the routines we follow. From sticky notes to mobile apps, memory aids can be simple yet incredibly effective for helping us retain information.

When I was preparing for my exams, I didn't always have the luxury of spending hours learning advanced memory techniques. So, I started using simple tools and habits that fit right into my daily routine. It was amazing how much these small tweaks helped me remember things better and stay organized.

Why Memory Aids Work

Memory aids work because they help take the pressure off your brain by externalizing some of the information. In other words, they provide reminders and cues so your brain doesn't have to work as hard to recall everything on its own. This reduces cognitive overload and makes it easier to remember important details when you need them.

Here's how you can start using everyday objects and routines to make memory-boosting part of your life.

1. Sticky Notes: The Power of Visual Reminders

One of the simplest yet most powerful tools for boosting memory is the humble sticky note. They're small, easy to place anywhere and serve as constant visual reminders.

How to Use Them:

- Write down key facts, dates, or concepts you need to remember on sticky notes.
- Place them in spots where you'll see them often—on your desk, fridge, bathroom mirror, or even your phone.
- Every time you see the note, read it out loud or visualize the concept to reinforce your memory.

Personal Example:

When I was preparing for the exams, I had sticky notes all over my house. In the morning, I'd see notes about important historical dates stuck to my bathroom mirror. I had to read notes of geography (Hills, Mountains, rivers, wetlands, national parks) pinned to the wall.

These constant visual cues kept the information fresh in my mind, even during routine tasks.

2. Flashcards: Quick and Efficient Learning

Flashcards are another tried-and-tested method for boosting memory. They help you engage in **active recall**, a powerful technique where you challenge your brain to remember information without looking at the answers first. Flashcards can be used for anything—definitions, key terms, dates, or formulas.

How to Use Them:

- Write a question or key concept on one side of the card and the answer or explanation on the other.
- Quiz yourself regularly. Flip through the flashcards, and for each one, try to recall the answer before looking.
- As you review, separate the cards into two piles: one for concepts you remember well and another for concepts you need to review more often.

Bonus Tip:

You can use mobile apps like **Anki** or **Quizlet** to create digital flashcards. These apps offer a spaced repetition system (SRS), which automatically schedules the cards for review based on how well you remember them. The cards you struggle with appear more frequently, while the ones you know well are shown less often.

I used flashcards extensively to remember key articles of the Indian Constitution and one-liner points. I had to Write the article number on one side and the details on the other & practice daily.

One of my friends, **Shivam**, used the Anki app during his preparation for the UPSC CSE Prelims 2024. As a software engineer, he uses technology effectively to boost his study efficiency. Even though he doesn't think of himself as very smart, I see his approach as part of a smart study. By using Anki's spaced repetition system (SRS), not to be confused with Software Requirements Specification (SRS) used in software development, he was able to retain more facts compared to traditional methods. The app repeats questions marked as difficult more frequently, reinforcing neural pathways until the correct answers become second nature.

> "*"Repetition is the mother of learning. But how you repeat information-especially through active recall determines how well you retain it."*"

3. Mindful Use of Your Smartphone

Your smartphone can be more than just a source of distraction—it can be a powerful memory aid. There are numerous apps designed to help you manage your study schedule, set reminders, and even review important information on the go.

How to Use It:

- **Reminders & Alarms**: Use your phone's alarm or reminder feature to set up study sessions, review times, or deadlines. You can even set it to remind you to review flashcards or go over key points throughout the day.
- **Notes App**: Use your phone's note-taking app to jot down important ideas or facts as soon as they come to mind. Reviewing these quick notes at the end of the day can help reinforce the information.
- **Voice Memos**: If you're tired of reading or writing, try recording key points and listening to them during a walk or while commuting.

I used to record voice memos of key facts and concepts I needed to memorize, like important Supreme Court judgments, FR, DPSP, FD, or key terms from economics like repo rate, CRR, SLR and Agriculture crops. I'd listen to them while walking or exercising, which allowed me to study without feeling like I was tied to my desk. It helped reinforce the information in a more relaxed setting.

4. The Memory Box: Grouping Similar Items

A **memory box** is a simple tool where you group related items or concepts in a single place. The idea is that when you see one item, it triggers your memory about the others. It's a way of physically linking ideas together, so your brain creates associations that are easier to recall.

How to Use It:

- Get a small box, folder, or space in your room and fill it with physical items related to the subjects you're studying. For example, you could place your notes, flashcards, and sticky notes about a single topic in one box.
- Whenever you sit down to study that subject, take out the box and go through everything inside. The physical act of collecting and reviewing the items helps create stronger mental connections between the concepts.

For geography, you can have a memory box with a world map, flashcards about important rivers and mountain ranges, and a set of notes on climatic patterns. Whenever you opened the box, the physical act of going through these materials helped you mentally organize the concepts, which made them easier to recall later.

5. The Power of Routines: Making Memory a Habit

Routines are another excellent way to boost your memory. By setting up consistent habits, you train your brain to retain information more easily. When you make something part of your routine, your brain becomes more efficient at processing and storing that information.

How to Create a Memory-Boosting Routine:

- **Morning Review**: Start your day by reading newspaper and reviewing the key concepts you need to remember. Spend 10–15 minutes going through flashcards, sticky notes, or a mind map. This primes your brain for learning throughout the day.
- **Nightly Recap**: Before going to bed, quickly review what you've learned that day. This reinforces the material while you sleep, a time when your brain consolidates memory.

- **Daily Quizzes**: Turn reviewing into a daily habit by quizzing yourself regularly. Set aside 5–10 minutes to test your memory on specific topics, using flashcards or mental recall.

Personal things:

In the mornings, I make a habit of making my bed and brushing my teeth with my non-dominant hand, which is different from my usual routine. Additionally, I practice writing the alphabet with my left hand. These activities help activate neurons and build new neural connections in the brain. Typically, when we use our right hand, the left hemisphere of the brain is more active, as it controls motor functions on the opposite side of the body. By regularly using the opposite hand, we engage the less dominant hemisphere, strengthening neural pathways.

Over time, with consistent practice, these neural pathways become stronger, leading to tasks being performed more efficiently. This process, known as **neuroplasticity** (we had discussed earlier), allows the brain to adapt and become more flexible. Eventually, the repeated action becomes so ingrained that it moves into **muscle memory**, requiring less conscious effort. For example, when locking a door for the first time, we pay close attention to each step. However, after repeated practice, the brain takes over, and the task becomes automatic, freeing us from having to focus intently on it.

> *"The beauty of neuroplasticity lies in its reminder that we are never stuck—we can always learn, adapt, and evolve."*

This ability of the brain to automate repetitive tasks is part of how we conserve cognitive energy, allowing us to focus on new challenges. It also highlights how engaging in activities that challenge our typical patterns can enhance brain flexibility and resilience.

I also review my notes every morning with a cup of tea. This simple, consistent routine ensured that I started my day with a focused mindset, and it helped me retain information better over time. Similarly, every night, I'd spend a few minutes recalling what I had studied throughout the day, which helped lock the information into my long-term memory.

6. Using Everyday Objects as Memory Triggers

You can also use everyday objects to serve as **memory triggers**. By associating certain objects with specific concepts, you create a cue that reminds you to recall information whenever you see that object.

How to Use It:

- Choose an object you see often (like a keychain, pen, or notebook) and mentally link it to a specific piece of information. Every time you see or use that object, try to recall that information.

- Changing objects or routines regularly keeps your brain engaged by forming new associations. For example, moving frequently used app icons like WhatsApp, Chrome, or Instagram to new locations on your phone can disrupt automatic habits. Initially, you might open the wrong app, but after a few attempts, your brain adapts and recognizes the change.

This practice retrains neural pathways, enhancing the brain's ability to learn and adapt. It strengthens **neuroplasticity**, improving *cognitive* flexibility and *focus* by breaking established patterns and forming new ones.

Incorporating simple memory aids into your daily routine can make a significant difference in your ability to retain information. Whether it's using sticky notes, flashcards, or your smartphone, the key is to externalize some of the pressure on your brain by using tools that provide reminders and triggers.

SIX

PHYSICAL ACTIVITY BOOSTS MEMORY

> *"Movement is a medicine for creating change in a person's physical, emotional, and mental states".*
> ***-Carol Welch***

When you think about improving your memory, you probably picture studying for hours with a book or using flashcards, right? But here's something surprising: **physical activity** can play a huge role in boosting your memory. Moving your body isn't just good for your muscles and heart—it's also great for your brain.

Many people, myself included, often underestimate the connection between exercise and memory. During my UPSC preparation and college times, I used to spend long hours sitting at my desk, thinking that staying still would help me focus better. But as I started integrating physical activity into my routine, I noticed a shift. Not only did I feel more energized, but I also began remembering information more effectively.

How Exercise Boosts Memory

The science behind this is fascinating. When you move your body, it increases **blood flow to the brain**, which in turn delivers more oxygen and nutrients. This stimulates the growth of **new brain cells** and strengthens the connections between neurons—essentially, it helps your brain stay sharp.

Exercise also releases **brain-derived neurotrophic factor (BDNF)**, which is like fertilizer for your brain cells. BDNF encourages the growth of new neurons and helps strengthen existing ones, making it easier for your brain to form and retain memories. In addition, exercise helps reduce stress, which can otherwise impair your ability to focus and remember.

The Types of Physical Activities That Help Memory

You don't need to be an athlete to get the brain benefits of exercise. Even light activities like walking or stretching can improve memory. Here are a few types of physical exercises you can integrate into your routine to help enhance memory retention:

1. **Aerobic Exercise**:
   Activities like walking, jogging, cycling, or swimming are great for getting your heart rate up, which in turn increases blood flow to the brain. Aerobic exercises are particularly effective for improving memory because they promote the growth of the hippocampus—the part of the brain responsible for memory.

I often take a brisk walk in the evening after studying. This not only gave me a break but also helped me process and retain what I had studied. Sometimes, I'd use the walk as a chance to mentally review key concepts, and I found that it helped cement the information in my mind.

1. **Strength Training**:
   Lifting weights or doing bodyweight exercises like push-ups or squats might not seem related to memory, but studies show that strength training can improve cognitive function as well. It helps boost **attention, learning, and long-term memory**

If I was feeling sluggish after a long study session, I had to take a few minutes to do some light strength exercises. A few push-ups or even stretching helped wake me up and get my mind back in gear. It's a great way to break up long periods of sitting and refocus your brain.

3. **Yoga and Stretching**:
   Yoga is an excellent way to combine physical activity with mindfulness, both of which improve memory. Certain yoga poses, like the **tree pose, SuryaNamaskar, Kapalbhati, or Anulom-Vilom** can increase blood flow to the brain and help reduce stress—two factors that can enhance your ability to remember information. 10-15 minutes of stretching and breathing exercises can improve concentration levels.

4. **Dancing**:
   Dancing is not just fun—it's also a fantastic way to improve memory. Learning new dance moves challenges your brain to remember sequences, which strengthens neural connections. Plus, it's a great way to combine physical movement with enjoyment, making it easier to stick with as a regular habit.

> "*"Take care of your body. It's the only place you have to live."* ***-Jim Rohn***"

How to Integrate Physical Activity into Your Study Routine

You don't need to dedicate hours to exercise to see the memory benefits. Incorporating small bursts of physical activity into your study routine can make a significant difference. Here are some practical ways to integrate movement into your daily schedule:

1. **Study Break Walks**:
   Take a 10-15 minute walk or tea break every few hours during study breaks. Not only will this give your brain a rest, but the movement will help refresh your mind and make it easier to remember what you've been studying.
2. **Stretch During Breaks**:
   If you're pressed for time, try doing some simple stretches between study sessions. Stretching helps improve circulation and gives your body a break from sitting, which can leave you feeling more alert and ready to tackle the next study session.
3. **Use Exercise as a Memory Review Tool**:
   You can combine exercise with reviewing your notes. For example, while jogging or walking, try mentally recalling key points or listen to your voice memo (discussed earlier) from your study material. This forces your brain to retrieve information while your body is moving, which helps strengthen memory recall.
4. **Quick Workouts to Break Up Study Time**:
   If you've been sitting for too long and feel your brain getting tired, do a quick 5-minute workout. It could be anything—jumping jacks, squats, or even light jogging in place. This brief burst of activity will wake you up and get the blood flowing back to your brain.

The Link Between Physical Activity and Sleep

One significant benefit of exercise is its positive impact on sleep, which is essential for memory consolidation. During sleep, your brain processes and organizes the information learned throughout the day, reinforcing what you've studied. I learned in my psychology optional how critical sleep is for this process. It's fascinating to note that growth hormone is released during sleep, facilitating development across various bodily functions. This may be the reason why doctors recommend patients to have sound sleep so that the body can be in the recovery phase.

Regular physical activity enhances sleep quality, allowing your brain to perform its crucial tasks more effectively. Better sleep not only improves memory retention but also supports overall cognitive function, emotional regulation, and physical health, making exercise a vital component of a well-rounded lifestyle.

It's easy to fall into the trap of thinking that the best way to improve memory is by cramming more study hours like 15-18 Hours. But the truth is, that physical activity can significantly enhance your memory by boosting blood flow to the brain, reducing stress, and promoting the growth of new brain cells.

You don't need to spend hours at the gym to see these benefits. Just incorporating small amounts of movement—whether it's a walk, a few stretches, or even dancing—can make a noticeable difference in how well you remember the information you're studying. So, the next time you're feeling stuck or mentally drained, take a break and move your body. Your brain will thank you for it!

SEVEN

The Pegging Technique: Organize Your Thoughts

> *"Order and simplification are the first steps toward the mastery of a subject."*
>
> ***-Thomas Mann***

Have you ever struggled to remember a list of items or a sequence of facts in the correct order? Whether it's a shopping list, key dates in history, or steps in a process, our brains often have trouble recalling things in the right order—unless we give it a little help. That's where the **pegging technique** comes in.

The pegging technique is a simple but effective memory tool that allows you to **link information to specific "pegs"** in your mind. These pegs act as anchors, helping you organize and recall information in a structured way. It's especially useful for memorizing lists, numbers, or even concepts that need to be remembered in a specific order.

During preparation, I found this technique invaluable for organizing and remembering the many lists I had to recall—like important constitutional articles, names of international organizations, and steps in scientific processes. The pegging technique turned memorization from a daunting task into something manageable and even fun.

How the Pegging Technique Works

The idea behind pegging is simple: you create a list of mental "pegs," or visual placeholders, that you can associate with the information you want to remember. Each peg is linked to a number or position, and you attach the information you want to remember to each peg. When you need to recall the information, you mentally go through the pegs in order, retrieving the details attached to each one. You can read the above paragraph again.

Visualise and think of it like hanging coats on a row of hooks. The hooks are always in the same place, and once you hang a coat on a hook, it's easy to come back and find it later. Similarly, with pegging, the pegs (or hooks) stay fixed in your mind, and you can "hang" new information on them whenever you need to memorize something.

Step-by-Step Guide to the Pegging Technique

Here's a step-by-step guide to using the pegging technique:

1. **Create a Set of Pegs**
   The first step is to create a list of pegs. These are visual markers that you'll associate with numbers or positions. The most common way to do this is to use **rhyming words** for each number. For example:

   1. One = Sun
   2. Two = Shoe
   3. Three = Tree
   4. Four = Door
   5. Five = Hive
   6. Six = Sticks
   7. Seven = Heaven
   8. Eight = Gate
   9. Nine = Vine
   10. Ten = Hen

These rhymes create vivid mental images that are easy to visualize. You can modify the pegs to suit your preferences—just make sure they're memorable and easy to visualize.

1. **Associate Information with Each Peg**
   Once you have your set of pegs, the next step is to associate the

information you want to remember with each peg. The key here is to create vivid, unusual, or even funny mental images that link the peg to the information. *The more bizarre or interesting the image, the easier it will be to remember.*

For example, if you're trying to remember a list of Indian states and their capitals, you could associate each state-capital pair with a peg:

- **One (Sun)**: Imagine a giant sun shining over Mumbai, the capital of Maharashtra. Picture the sun setting over the Gateway of India.
- **Two (Shoe)**: Picture a giant shoe stepping into Bengaluru, the capital of Karnataka. Maybe the shoe is leaving footprints on the city's famous gardens.
- **Three (Tree)**: Visualize a tree growing out of the middle of Bhopal, the capital of Madhya Pradesh. Imagine the branches spreading over the entire city.

By linking each peg to a specific piece of information, you create a mental map that's much easier to recall. It may be hard to create but it is effective.

3. **Practice and Review**
   Like any memory technique, the pegging technique works best with practice. After you've created your pegs and associated them with information, go over them a few times in your mind. Visualize each peg and the image you've attached to it. This mental rehearsal helps strengthen the connections in your brain.

The more often you practice, the easier it becomes to recall the information. And the best part is, you can reuse the same set of pegs for different lists. Once you've mastered the technique, it becomes a versatile tool for all kinds of memory tasks.

Example: Using Pegging for Exam Preparation

Let's say you're preparing for a competitive exam and need to memorize a list of historical events in order. Here's how you can use the pegging technique:

1. **One (Sun)**: The First War of Indian Independence in 1857. Picture a bright sun shining over a battlefield, with soldiers from both sides fighting

under its heat.

2. **Two (Shoe)**: The Non-Cooperation Movement of 1920. Imagine a pair of shoes marching in a protest, symbolizing Gandhi's movement.
3. **Three (Tree)**: The Salt March of 1930. Visualize Gandhi walking with a tree made of salt, as if he's leading a march to a giant salt tree on the beach.

These vivid images linked to pegs make it easier to remember events and their order. When you're in an exam and need to recall the list, you can mentally walk through the pegs and retrieve the associated information. During school or college exams, it often feels like you're visualizing a specific page in a book; for instance, you might see text on the left side, but if the image is blurry, it indicates that the neural connections are not strong enough, possibly due to a lack of revision.

Solution with pegging, when I needed to remember key events in the freedom struggle, I used the rhyme pegs and visualized images like Gandhi leading a shoe march for the Non-Cooperation Movement or the sun shining over the battlefield of 1857. These images were not only memorable but also helped me recall the order of events accurately.

Why the Pegging Technique Works

The pegging technique works for several reasons:

- **Engages Your Imagination**: By creating vivid, unusual images, you engage the creative part of your brain. This makes the information more interesting and memorable.
- **Uses Visual and Spatial Memory**: Our brains are excellent at remembering visual and spatial information. By attaching abstract facts to concrete images, you make them easier to recall.
- **Creates a Structured Path**: The pegs act as a mental framework or structure that you can follow. Instead of trying to remember random bits of information, you're following a clear sequence, which makes recall easier.

Tips for Mastering the Pegging Technique

- **Make the Images Personal**: The more personal or emotional your images, the more likely you are to remember them. Don't be afraid to get creative and make the images silly or exaggerated—that's what makes them stick.

- **Review Regularly**: As with any memory technique, *regular review is key*. Go over your pegs and associations daily or weekly to keep them fresh in your mind.
- **Start Small**: If you're new to the pegging technique, start with small lists (like grocery items or a few key facts) and gradually work your way up to more complex lists.

The pegging technique is a powerful memory tool that can help you organize your thoughts and remember information in a structured, reliable way. Whether you're preparing for an exam, trying to remember a sequence of steps, or just want to keep track of a list, pegging can make the task much easier.

Once you get the hang of it, you'll find that pegging isn't just useful for academic purposes—it's a practical tool for daily life as well. From remembering to-do lists to organizing complex information, the pegging technique gives your brain a clear path to follow.

EIGHT

FOUNDATIONS OF MEMORY: BUILDING STRONG STUDY HABITS

> *"We are what we repeatedly do. Excellence, then, is not an act but a habit."* - ***Aristotle***

No matter how many memory techniques you learn, the foundation of a strong memory lies in good study habits. Think of your brain like a house—no matter how beautifully you decorate the rooms, the structure will only be as strong as its foundation. The same goes for memory: without solid study habits, it's much harder to retain and recall information in the long run.

As I prepared for my exams, I realized that memory techniques were only part of the puzzle. I had to establish consistent habits—regular study sessions, smart note-taking, and proper review cycles—to ensure that what I learned stayed with me. In this chapter, I'll walk you through the habits that made all the difference in my preparation and how you can use them to strengthen your learning process.

1. Create a Consistent Study Schedule

The brain thrives on routine. When you study at the same time every day, you train your brain to expect and prepare for learning. This consistency not only makes it easier to focus, but it also helps with memory retention because your brain knows when to switch into "learning mode."

How to Create a Study Schedule:

- **Block Out Study Times**: Pick specific times each day when you'll focus on studying. Make these times consistent, whether it's in the morning, afternoon, or evening. It's important to find a time when you're naturally more focused and alert.
- **Mix Subjects**: Instead of studying the same subject for hours on end, mix things up. For example, if you're preparing for an exam like UPSC, you can study Indian history in the morning, move on to geography in the afternoon, and wrap up with a revision of both in the evening. This variety keeps your brain engaged and reduces burnout.
- **Use the Pomodoro Technique**: Studying in 25-minute focused sessions with short breaks can help you maintain concentration. After every 25 minutes of study, take a 5-minute break to refresh your brain. After four Pomodoro (two hours), take a longer break (15-30 minutes).

2. Break Down Big Goals into Small, Manageable Tasks

One of the biggest challenges during exam preparation is feeling overwhelmed by the sheer volume of material. But here's a simple truth: **big goals are best achieved by breaking them down into smaller, manageable tasks**. When you divide a large subject into smaller chunks, your brain processes it more easily, and you're less likely to feel stressed.

How to Break Down Your Study Material:

- **Make a Study Plan**: Divide your syllabus into smaller units. Instead of saying, "I'll study history today," break it down into specific chapters or topics, like "Today, I'll focus on the Vijaynagar Empire and the Peasants movement in modern history." This makes the task feel more manageable and gives you a sense of accomplishment when you complete each section.
- **Set Daily or Weekly Goals**: Once you've divided your material into smaller units, set daily or weekly goals. For example, aim to complete two chapters of economics this week, or review key points in Indian polity over the weekend.
- **Track Your Progress**: Keeping track of your progress is crucial. Use a checklist or a planner to mark off what you've studied. Seeing how much you've accomplished boosts motivation and keeps you on course.

3. Active Learning: Engage, Don't Just Read

It's easy to fall into the trap of passive reading—just skimming through pages of notes or textbooks without truly understanding or engaging with the material. But memory works best when you actively engage with what you're learning. **Active learning** means interacting with the material—asking questions, summarizing, teaching it to someone else, or applying it in practical ways.

How to Use Active Learning:

- **Ask Questions**: As you read, ask yourself questions about the material. Why is this concept important? How does it relate to something else I've learned? This encourages your brain to process the information deeply.
- **Summarize in Your Own Words**: After reading a section, close the book and try to summarize what you've learned in your own words. This forces your brain to process and organize the material, making it easier to remember.
- **Teach What You Learn**: One of the most effective ways to reinforce memory is to teach the material to someone else. When you explain concepts to others, you have to organize your thoughts clearly, which strengthens your understanding and recall.

4. Take Good Notes: The Cornell Method

Good note-taking is a cornerstone of effective studying. When you take notes in a structured way, it helps your brain organize the information, making it easier to review and remember later. One of the best note-taking methods is the **Cornell Method**, which is designed to help you review and recall information efficiently.

How to Use the Cornell Method:

- **Divide Your Page**: Create a margin on the left side of your notebook (about 1/3 of the width of the page). The larger section on the right is where you'll take your notes, while the smaller left section is for cues and key points.
- **Take Notes in the Right Section**: As you study, write down the key points, definitions, and explanations in the main right section.
- **Write Cues in the Left Section**: After your study session, go back and fill in the left section with cues—questions, keywords, or phrases that summarize the main ideas. These cues will help you recall the

information when reviewing.

- **Summarize at the Bottom**: Leave a few lines at the bottom of the page for a summary of the notes. This helps consolidate the information and provides a quick overview for later review

5. The Power of Review: Spaced Repetition

One of the most important aspects of memory retention is regular review. You can't expect to remember something if you only look at it once. The technique of **spaced repetition** involves reviewing material at increasing intervals over time, which helps move information from short-term to long-term memory.

How to Use Spaced Repetition:

- **Initial Review**: Review new information within 24 hours of first learning it. This reinforces the memory while it's still fresh.
- **Second Review**: Review the material again 2-3 days later to strengthen the memory further.
- **Subsequent Reviews**: Continue reviewing the information at longer intervals—once a week, then once every two weeks, and so on. The idea is to review it before you forget it, but not so frequently that you waste time repeating information you already know.

6. Sleep: The Hidden Key to Memory

One often overlooked aspect of memory is sleep. **Sleep is crucial for memory consolidation**, the process by which your brain organizes and stores the information you've learned throughout the day. Without enough sleep, your brain struggles to process and retain new information.

How to Improve Sleep for Better Memory:

- **Stick to a Sleep Schedule**: Try to go to bed and wake up at the same time every day, even on weekends. This helps regulate your body's internal clock and improves the quality of your sleep.
- **Create a Bedtime Routine**: Wind down before bed with calming activities like reading (something not related to your studies), light stretching, or meditation.
- **Limit Screen Time**: Avoid using electronic devices, especially your phone, for at least 30 minutes before bedtime. The blue light emitted by screens can disrupt your sleep cycle.

During my preparation, I made sure to get enough sleep, even during crunch times. I noticed that on days when I stayed up late to study, I'd struggle to recall information the next day. But when I stuck to a regular sleep schedule, my memory was sharper, and I retained more of what I had learned.

Good study habits form the foundation of effective learning and long-term memory. Whether it's creating a consistent study schedule, using active learning techniques, or making time for review, these habits help your brain organize and retain information in a way that sticks. Memory is like a muscle—the more you use it, the stronger it gets, but it needs the right routine to thrive.

NINE

Connecting Ideas: The Key to Better Understanding and Recall

> *"The more that you read, the more things you will know. The more that you learn, the more places you'll go."*- ***Dr. Seuss***

Memory is not just about stuffing information into your brain. It's about making connections. When you link new information to something you already know, it becomes much easier to understand and remember. This is where the power of **connecting ideas** comes into play.

Think of your brain as a vast network of roads. Each piece of knowledge is like a city, and the more roads that connect to that city, the easier it is to get there. When you learn something new in isolation, it's like a city with only one road leading to it. But when you link that knowledge to other ideas, you create multiple pathways, making it easier to recall the information when you need it.

Why Connecting Ideas Works

Our brains are wired to think in connections. When we learn something new, our brain naturally tries to relate it to existing knowledge. This process of making associations not only helps with understanding but also strengthens memory because it creates multiple pathways to the information.

Here's how connecting ideas benefits memory:

- **Improves Comprehension**: By linking new information to what you already know, you create a deeper understanding of the material. This helps your brain store the information in long-term memory.
- **Creates Mental Hooks**: When you connect ideas, each piece of knowledge acts as a "hook" for the next, making it easier to retrieve the information when you need it.
- **Reduces Cognitive Overload**: Instead of memorizing isolated facts, linking ideas allows you to remember concepts as part of a larger, connected framework, which reduces the mental strain of learning.

How to Connect Ideas for Better Memory

1. **Use Analogies and Comparisons**

One of the most effective ways to link new information to something you already know is by using **analogies** or comparisons. Analogies help you understand new concepts by comparing them to something familiar, creating a bridge between the old and the new.

Let's say you're trying to understand the concept of federalism in Indian polity. If you've already studied the structure of a corporation, you could compare federalism to a company where the central government is like the headquarters, and the state governments are like the regional branches. This analogy creates a clear mental image that makes it easier to grasp and remember how federalism works.

1. **Create Mind Maps**

A **mind map** is a visual tool that helps you connect ideas by organizing them into a web of related concepts. This is one of the best ways to see the relationships between different pieces of information, especially when you're dealing with a large amount of material.

How to Create a Mind Map:

- Start with a central idea in the middle of the page. This could be a key concept or a subject, like "Indian Polity."

- From the central idea, draw branches that represent subtopics, such as "Constitution," "Fundamental Rights," and "Executive."
- For each subtopic, add smaller branches that represent key details. For example, under "Executive," you might have "President," "Prime Minister," and "Cabinet."

By visually mapping out the connections between ideas, you create a structure that helps your brain organize and recall the information more easily.

Personal views:

Mind mapping was a game-changer for me. Study the physical, cultural, political, and economic geography of an area to gain a comprehensive understanding of how its environment operates.

Next, focus on the key environmental features in each region, including climate, vegetation, soil, water resources, and air quality. By creating mind maps with these elements, you can better understand how they interact and influence the overall functioning of the environment, shaping both human activities and ecological processes.

Link New Information to Personal Experiences

One of the most powerful ways to make information memorable is to connect it to your own experiences. When you relate a concept to something personal, it becomes emotionally charged, which makes it stick in your memory more effectively.

> "*"Memory works best when it's connected to something else. The more associations you create, the easier it is to retrieve information."*"

Example:

If you're learning about the various types of taxes in economics (direct vs. indirect taxes), think about how these taxes apply to your life. Have you ever paid income tax (direct)? What about sales tax on items you've bought (indirect)? By linking abstract concepts to real-life examples, you create a more meaningful connection that's easier to recall.

4. **Use the Feynman Technique**

Named after the famous physicist Richard Feynman, the **Feynman Technique** is a simple method for connecting ideas and improving understanding. The idea is to take a complex topic and explain it as if you're teaching it to a child. This forces you to break the concept down into simple, relatable terms, which helps solidify your understanding and reveals any gaps in your knowledge.

How to Use the Feynman Technique:

- Pick a topic you're studying.
- Imagine you have to teach this topic to someone who has no background knowledge—like a child or a friend or to your grandmother.
- Simplify the explanation as much as possible. Use analogies, examples, and simple language.
- If you struggle to explain a concept clearly, go back to your notes and review until you understand it well enough to teach it..

5. **Draw Parallels Between Different Subjects**

Sometimes, the best way to connect ideas is by finding links between different subjects. Many topics overlap across disciplines, and recognizing these parallels can help you understand both subjects better.

Example:

If you're studying environmental geography and economics, you can link the concept of **sustainable development** in geography to **economic growth** models in economics. Understanding how environmental policies affect economic development creates a broader, more connected understanding of both subjects.

6. **Tell a Story**

We've already touched on the power of storytelling in previous chapters, but it's worth mentioning again: **telling a story** is one of the best ways to connect ideas and make them more memorable. When you weave facts and concepts into a narrative, your brain organizes them into a logical sequence, which makes them easier to remember.

Example:

If you're studying the events leading up to India's independence, try turning it into a story. Imagine the key figures like Mahatma Gandhi, Jawaharlal Nehru, and Subhash Chandra Bose, Bhagat Singh as characters in a narrative. What were their motivations? What challenges did they face?

By telling the story of India's freedom struggle in a way that feels personal and emotional, you'll create strong connections that help you recall the details more easily.

Thoughts on Connecting Ideas

Connecting ideas is one of the most powerful tools you can use to improve memory and understanding. By linking new information to what you already know—whether through analogies, mind maps, personal experiences, or storytelling—you create a web of associations that makes it easier to recall the material later.

Instead of seeing facts as isolated pieces of information, start viewing them as parts of a larger, interconnected system. This not only helps with retention but also deepens your comprehension, making learning a more engaging and rewarding process.

TEN

Remembering Names: How to Never Forget a Face Again

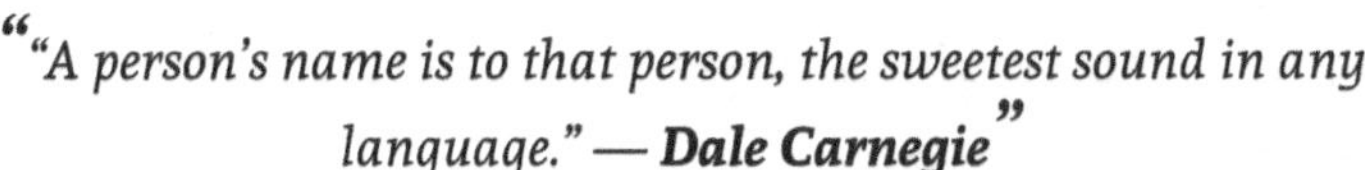

> *"A person's name is to that person, the sweetest sound in any language."* — ***Dale Carnegie***

We've all been there—introduced to someone at an event or gathering, only to forget their name moments later. It's a common problem, but forgetting names can sometimes feel awkward, especially in important social or professional situations. Fortunately, remembering names and faces is a skill you can develop with the right techniques.

Why We Forget Names

Before diving into the techniques, let's understand why we often forget names in the first place. The problem usually isn't memory—it's **attention.** When we're introduced to someone, we're often focused on other things—our next words, the situation, or the conversation. As a result, the name simply doesn't "stick" because we didn't fully register it in the first place.

The key to remembering names is focus and creating a connection. By paying closer attention and using visualization or association, you can link the name to something memorable and make it easier to recall later.

Techniques for Remembering Names

1. **Repeat the Name Immediately**

The simplest way to remember someone's name is to say it out loud as soon as you hear it. Repeating the name immediately helps reinforce it in your mind. This also gives you a moment to make sure you've heard the name correctly.

Example:

When someone says, "Hi, I'm Abhay," respond with, "Nice to meet you, Abhay." This small act of repeating the name helps strengthen the memory.

If it's a group introduction, try to repeat everyone's name as you meet them: "This is Kajal, Neeraj, Abhishek, and Sakshi." Even if you're just repeating it in your head, the act of mentally reviewing the names helps.

1. **Make a Visual Association**

One of the most effective techniques for remembering names is to make a **visual association.** This means creating a mental image that links the person's name to something familiar or easy to picture. Your brain is excellent at remembering images, so when you link a name to a vivid mental image, it's more likely to stick.

How to Use This Technique:

- When someone introduces themselves, think of a strong visual image that connects to their name. The more unique or vivid, the better.
- For example, if you meet someone named **Ravi**, you could imagine them holding a giant sunflower (since "Ravi" means "sun" in Sanskrit). If you meet someone named **Neha**, you might picture them surrounded by raindrops (since "Neha" sounds like "neh," meaning rain in Hindi).

Example:

I often used this technique during group meetings or study sessions. For example, I once met a person named Deepak, and I mentally pictured him holding a bright oil lamp (as "Deepak" means lamp in Hindi). This association made it much easier for me to recall his name during the conversation.

3. **Link the Name to Something Personal**

Another powerful strategy is to link the name to something personal or familiar. This could be a friend or family member who shares the same name, or even a celebrity with that name. Making this connection helps solidify the name in your memory because you're tying it to something you already know.

How to Use This Technique:

- When someone introduces themselves, quickly think of someone you know with the same name.
- For example, if you meet someone named **Sanjay**, you could mentally link them to a friend or family member who has the same name, or even to actor Sanjay Dutt if that's easier for you.
- If you meet someone named **Anjali**, you might associate them with the character Anjali from the famous Bollywood movie *Kuch Kuch Hota Hai*. This mental link helps trigger the name whenever you see the person.

4. **Use Mnemonics**

A **mnemonic** is a memory tool that helps you remember information through a simple phrase, rhyme, or wordplay. For names, you can create a mnemonic by associating the person's name with a defining feature or characteristic.

How to Use This Technique:

- When you meet someone, create a short rhyme or wordplay that links their name to something memorable about them.
- For example, if you meet someone named **Devesh**, and they're wearing a Dark Blue shirt, you could create a mental phrase like "Devesh in Dark Blue."
- If you meet a person named **Manisha** and they have curly hair, you could make a mental note: "Manisha with vibrant curls." This rhyme sticks in your mind and helps you remember both the name and the person's appearance.

5. **Ask for the Name's Spelling or Meaning**

If you're introduced to someone whose name you didn't catch clearly, don't be afraid to ask for clarification. Asking how to spell or pronounce their name not only shows that you're paying attention but also gives your brain another chance to lock the name in.

How to Use This Technique:

- Politely ask, "How do you spell your name?" or "Can you tell me what your name means?"
- This shows that you're genuinely interested in getting their name right and gives you a mental image to help remember it.

If someone says their name is **Aslay**, you could ask, "Is that spelled with an 'A' at the beginning?" or "What does your name mean?" Engaging with the name in this way creates a stronger memory trace.

Tip:
Asking for the meaning of names helped me a lot when meeting people with less common names. For example, I met a person named Prajakta, and when I asked about the meaning, I learned that it's the name of a flower. That association helped me remember her name long after our first meeting.

6. **Use the Name During the Conversation**

To reinforce the name further, try using it during the conversation. This not only helps solidify the name in your memory but also makes the other person feel acknowledged and respected.

How to Use This Technique:

- During the conversation, use the person's name naturally. For example, you could say, "That's a great point, Monica" or "Tell me more about your work, Priya."
- Using the name a few times without overdoing it will strengthen the connection in your mind.

The Power of Combining Techniques

You don't have to stick to just one technique—often, combining methods works best. For example, you could repeat the name immediately, then create a visual association, and follow up by using the name in conversation. By using multiple techniques, you reinforce the memory from different angles, making it much harder to forget.

Thoughts on Remembering Names

Remembering names is a skill that improves with practice, and by using these simple techniques, you can become much better at it. Whether it's repeating the name, making a visual association, or linking it to something personal, the key is to pay attention and create connections in your mind.

Mastering the art of remembering names is not just a memory exercise—it's also a valuable social skill that can help you build better relationships, both personally and professionally.

ELEVEN

MASTERING NUMBERS: TECHNIQUES TO RECALL NUMERICAL DATA

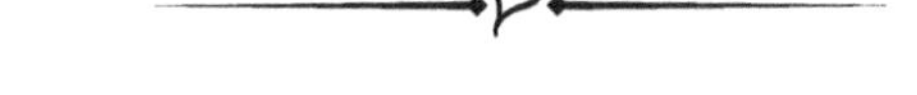

> *"Numbers have life; they're not just symbols on paper."*
> **—Shakuntala Devi**

Numbers are everywhere, whether it's phone numbers, exam scores, historical dates, or statistics. But for many people, numbers are among the hardest things to remember. The reason for this is simple: numbers are abstract. They don't naturally evoke images or emotions the way words or names do, which makes them more difficult for our brains to store and retrieve.

But just like with names and facts, you can use specific techniques to make numbers stick.

Why Numbers Are Hard to Remember

As I mentioned earlier, the human brain is wired to remember images and stories more easily than abstract data. Numbers, by nature, don't immediately form mental images. When you hear a random string of numbers, your brain struggles to find meaning or patterns, which is why they often slip away so quickly.

The key to remembering numbers is to **transform them into something meaningful**—whether through visualization, patterns, or associations. Once you can "see" the numbers as something concrete, they become much easier to remember.

Techniques for Remembering Numbers

1. **The Chunking Method**

One of the most effective ways to remember long strings of numbers is by breaking them down into smaller, manageable chunks. This technique, known as **chunking**, takes advantage of your brain's ability to remember groups of information more easily than individual pieces.

How to Use Chunking:

- Instead of trying to remember a long sequence of numbers like **194719852014**, break it down into smaller groups, like **1947 – 1985 – 2014**. By turning the number into three chunks, it's much easier to remember.
- This method works well for phone numbers, dates, and any other long sequence of numbers.

Example:

If you're trying to remember the number **177618471947**, it might feel overwhelming at first. But if you break it into chunks like **1776** (American Independence), **1847** (a famous year in history), and **1947** (Indian Independence), each group becomes associated with something familiar, making the sequence easier to recall.

During my preparation, I often had to memorize historical dates and numbers related to economic data. Instead of memorizing these numbers as a whole, I broke them into smaller parts. For example, if I needed to remember the year **1757** (Battle of Plassey) and **1947** (Independence of India), I'd connect these dates with major events, which made recalling them easier during the exam.

1. **The Number-Rhyme Method**

The **number rhyme method** is a simple but effective way to remember small sets of numbers (usually up to 10) by associating each number with a word that rhymes with it. You then create a mental image that links the rhyme word to the information you need to remember.

How to Use the Number-Rhyme Method:

- First, create rhymes for the numbers 1 to 10. For example:
  - 1 = Bun
  - 2 = Shoe
  - 3 = Tree
  - 4 = Door
  - 5 = Hive
  - 6 = Sticks
  - 7 = Heaven
  - 8 = Gate
  - 9 = Vine
  - 10 = Hen
- Next, link the rhyming word to the number you need to remember. For example, if you need to remember the number **42**, you could picture a **shoe** kicking open a **door** (since "2" rhymes with "shoe" and "4" rhymes with "door").

Example:

If you're trying to remember the number **27**, you could visualize a **shoe** (2) flying through the air and landing in **heaven** (7). The more vivid and imaginative the image, the more likely you are to remember the number.

3. **The Major System for Remembering Long Numbers**

For longer sequences of numbers, one of the most powerful techniques is the **Major System**. This method converts numbers into consonant sounds, which can then be turned into words. Once the numbers are turned into words, they become much easier to visualize and remember.

How the Major System Works:

- Each digit from 0 to 9 is assigned a consonant sound:
  - 0 = S or Z
  - 1 = T or D

  - 2 = N
  - 3 = M
  - 4 = R
  - 5 = L
  - 6 = J, SH, or CH
  - 7 = K or G
  - 8 = F or V
  - 9 = P or B

- To remember a number, you convert the digits into consonants and then create a word using vowels. For example, the number **32** can be converted to the sounds **M** (for 3) and **N** (for 2), which could form the word "moon."
- Once you've created a word, visualize it in a vivid mental image.

Example:

To remember the number **1947** (the year of India's independence), you could break it down using the Major System:

- 1 = T/D
- 9 = P/B
- 4 = R
- 7 = K/G
- You could form the word **"Tarp"** (T for 1, P for 9, R for 4, K for 7) and imagine a giant tarp covering the celebration of Indian Independence.

4. **The Memory Palace for Numbers**

You may already be familiar with the **memory palace technique** from earlier chapters, but it's also incredibly useful for remembering numbers. A memory palace involves creating a mental map of a familiar location (like your home) and placing pieces of information at different spots within that space. You can use this method to store numbers as well by associating them with specific locations.

How to Use the Memory Palace for Numbers:

- Choose a familiar location, such as your home or school.
- Assign each room or area a number.

- Place the number you need to remember in a specific location by linking it to a mental image. For example, you could visualize the number **52** as a giant **hive** (5) filled with **shoes** (2) sitting in your kitchen.

Example:

If you need to remember the number **1789** (the year of the French Revolution), you could imagine walking into your living room and seeing a **tree** (3) growing from a **bun** (1) while people are dancing in revolutionary costumes.

5. **Link Numbers to Personal Experiences**

Another powerful technique is to link numbers to your personal life. By associating a number with something meaningful to you—like a birthday, anniversary, or significant event—you create an emotional connection that makes it easier to remember.

How to Use This Technique:

- When you come across a number you need to remember, think about how it might relate to something personal. For example, if you need to remember the number **22**, you might associate it with your friend's birthday on the 22nd of a month.
- The stronger the emotional connection, the easier it will be to recall the number.

Example:

If you're trying to remember the number **1942**, you might link it to your grandmother's birth year or a family story from that period. One of my friend's birthdays is on 18 July and mine on the 9th then I used to remember 9x2=18. The personal connection makes the number more memorable.

Numbers don't have to be a source of frustration. By using techniques like chunking, the number rhyme method, the Major System, and the memory palace, you can transform numbers from abstract figures into memorable images and stories. These strategies make it easier to remember everything from historical dates to phone numbers and statistics.

TWELVE

ART OF MEMORY TO BOOST CREATIVITY AND LEARNING

> "Creativity is intelligence having fun."
> —***Albert Einstein***

While memory is often seen as a technical skill, it's also a highly creative process. Engaging your imagination can transform even the most mundane facts into something memorable and fun.

The **art of memory** is not a new concept. It dates back to ancient times when orators and scholars used imaginative memory techniques to recall long speeches, poems, and texts. They relied on mental imagery, vivid associations, and storytelling to bring abstract information to life, making it easier to remember.

By blending creativity with traditional memory techniques, you can make studying not only more effective but also more engaging. Whether you're preparing for exams or simply trying to retain more information in your daily life, these creative strategies can help you turn learning into an exciting process.

Why Creativity Enhances Memory

Our brains are naturally wired to respond to stories, images, and emotions. When you engage your imagination and turn information into something visual or narrative, you activate multiple parts of your brain. This strengthens the neural connections that make memories stick.

Here's why creativity helps with memory:

- **Engages Multiple Senses**: By visualizing, hearing, and feeling the information, you activate different areas of your brain, which enhances retention.
- **Makes Learning Fun**: Turning information into stories or images makes the process more enjoyable, reducing the monotony of rote memorization.
- **Creates Emotional Connections**: Imagination often triggers emotions, and research shows that emotional experiences are more likely to be remembered.

Creative Techniques to Enhance Memory

1. **Turn Information into Stories**

One of the most effective ways to remember information is to weave it into a **story**. Stories give meaning and structure to facts, making them easier to recall. You can use this technique for anything—historical events, scientific concepts, or even complex mathematical formulas.

How to Turn Facts into Stories:

- Start with the key pieces of information you need to remember.
- Create a storyline around those facts. Make the characters and plot vivid and engaging. The more detailed and imaginative, the better.
- Link the facts in a logical sequence that helps you recall them in order.

Example:

If you're studying the causes of World War II, you could turn the events into a narrative where each country is a character with specific motivations. Germany might be portrayed as a character seeking revenge for past losses (Treaty of Versailles), while Britain could be depicted as a cautious figure trying to maintain peace. By framing the events as a story with characters and a plot, it becomes easier to remember the details.

1. **Use Visual Metaphors and Imagery**

Another powerful memory technique is to create **visual metaphors** for abstract concepts. A visual metaphor links an idea to something tangible and easy to picture. By turning abstract information into images, you create mental hooks that make the material easier to recall.

How to Use Visual Metaphors:

- Identify the key concept you want to remember.
- Think of a visual metaphor that represents that concept. The more unusual or vivid, the better.
- Picture the metaphor in your mind and link it to the information you need to recall.

If you're studying the concept of **gravity**, you could picture it as a giant magnet pulling objects down to Earth. Whenever you think of gravity, this mental image of a magnet helps reinforce the idea.

When I was studying political systems, I visualized the **separation of powers** as a three-legged stool, where each leg represented one branch of government (executive, legislature, judiciary). The stool remained balanced only when all three legs were strong and independent. This metaphor made the concept of checks and balances easier to remember.

3. **Use the Memory Palace with Artistic Elements**

The **memory palace technique**, as we've discussed in earlier chapters, is a powerful tool for storing and recalling information. But when you combine this method with artistic elements—like colorful mental images or emotionally charged scenes—you amplify its effectiveness.

How to Use Artistic Imagery in Your Memory Palace:

- Choose a familiar location (your house, a park, or even a favorite place from childhood).
- Visualize the information as vivid, colorful objects or scenes placed around the location.
- Make the images as creative and detailed as possible. For example, instead of just visualizing a book to represent knowledge, you could picture a giant, glowing book with pages that turn themselves.

Example:

If you need to remember a list of famous inventions, imagine walking through your house and seeing each invention as a dramatic scene in different rooms. In your kitchen, you might see **Thomas Edison** inventing the light bulb, with sparks flying everywhere. In the living room, you could picture **Alexander Graham Bell** making the first telephone call, with phones ringing around the room.

4. **Create Mnemonic Poems or Songs**

Turning information into a **poem, rhyme, or song** is another creative way to make it more memorable. Rhymes and rhythms are easier for the brain to remember because they create a pattern. Plus, the process of creating a poem or song forces you to engage with the material more deeply.

How to Use This Technique:

- Take the key information you need to remember and turn it into a short poem or song.
- Focus on creating a rhyme or rhythm that makes the information stick.
- Sing or recite the poem to yourself regularly to reinforce the memory.

Example:

If you're trying to memorize the planets of the solar system in order, you could create a simple rhyme like:
"My Very Eager Mother Just Served Us Nachos" (Mercury, Venus, Earth, Mars, Jupiter, Saturn, Uranus, Neptune).
This turns an abstract list into a memorable, rhythmic phrase.

5. **Engage Emotionally with the Material**

Studies show that **emotionally charged memories** are more likely to be retained. If you can find a way to connect emotionally with the material—whether through personal experiences, stories, or imagination—you're more likely to remember it.

How to Use Emotional Engagement:

- As you study, try to connect the information to something personal or meaningful. Ask yourself: Why does this matter to me? How does it relate to my life or the world around me?

- Visualize the material in a way that triggers emotions—whether it's excitement, curiosity, or empathy.
- If you're studying historical events, imagine what it would have felt like to be there. If you're learning about scientific discoveries, think about the sense of wonder or curiosity that drove those breakthroughs.

If you're studying World War II, try imagining what it would have been like to live through that period. Picture yourself as a young person during the war, experiencing the fear, hope, and resilience that people felt at the time. This emotional connection makes the facts more real and easier to remember.

Thoughts on the Art of Memory

The art of memory is about turning information into something vibrant, meaningful, and fun. By using creativity and imagination, you can transform even the most complex topics into something engaging and memorable. Whether through storytelling, visual metaphors, rhymes, or emotional connections, these techniques not only make learning more effective but also more enjoyable.

Remember, your brain is like a canvas, and the more creatively you paint your memories, the more likely they are to stick. With these tools in your memory toolkit, you'll be able to recall information with ease and make learning an exciting process.

THIRTEEN
CONCLUSION

The Journey of Learning and Memory

As we've explored throughout this book, memory is not just a passive process of storing information—it's an active, creative skill that you can develop and refine over time. Whether you're preparing for competitive exams, trying to retain more from your daily readings, or simply looking to improve your recall abilities, the techniques we've covered can make a significant difference.

Reflecting on the Journey

From understanding how memory works at a scientific level to learning the art of visualization, storytelling, and connecting ideas, we've seen that memory is a flexible and dynamic process. It's not about being born with a good memory—it's about **building habits** that strengthen your brain's ability to store and retrieve information. Through focus, mindfulness, physical activity, and memory aids, you can transform your approach to learning and achieve better results in whatever you set your mind to.

My own journey—from struggling with memorization during my preparation to getting started these techniques—has shown me that anyone can improve their memory. It's not about talent; it's about using the right tools and strategies to make learning more effective and enjoyable.

Applying These Techniques to Your Life

The techniques we've discussed in this book are designed to be practical and easy to integrate into your daily life. Whether it's using the **pegging method** to organize information, creating vivid mental images through **visualization**, or turning facts into stories, each strategy is meant to make learning more engaging and manageable.

- Start by incorporating **focus exercises** into your study routine, using tools like the **Pomodoro technique** to stay sharp and attentive.
- Use **visualization** and **storytelling** to turn abstract concepts into something vivid and memorable.
- Strengthen your memory with physical activity, spacing out your review sessions, and breaking down complex ideas into **mind maps** or simple diagrams.

Remember, these techniques aren't just for exams—they're lifelong tools that can help you in every area of learning, from professional development to personal growth.

Embrace the Process

One of the most important lessons I've learned is that improving memory is a journey, not a destination. It's a skill that requires practice, patience, and consistency. There will be times when you forget things, struggle to recall information, or feel overwhelmed by the amount of material you need to learn. But that's okay—it's all part of the process.

By embracing these techniques and making them a part of your learning routine, you'll not only improve your memory but also develop a deeper understanding of the material you're studying. As you continue to practice these methods, you'll find that learning becomes easier, faster, and more enjoyable.

Final Thoughts:

Your brain is capable of amazing things, and by using the memory techniques in this book, you can unlock its full potential. Whether it's mastering subjects for an exam, remembering important details in your personal life, or expanding your general knowledge, these strategies will help you retain information more effectively and achieve your learning goals.

The journey of learning never truly ends—it's an ongoing process of growth and discovery. With the tools you now have, you're better equipped to tackle any challenge that comes your way. So, go ahead—apply these methods, experiment with them, and continue building the skill of memory. You'll be amazed at what you can achieve.

Thank you for taking this journey with me. May your path of learning be filled with curiosity, creativity, and the joy of discovery!

About Author

Abhit Tomar holds a master's degree from the University of Delhi and has pursued competitive exams, including the Civil Services Examination and various State Public Service Commission (PCS) exams, with psychology as his optional subject. Initially a tech enthusiast, Abhit's passion for exploring how technology intersects with human cognition and learning led him to a deeper interest in cognitive science and brain optimization techniques.

Transitioning from a tech background to becoming a writer, Abhit has dedicated his work to understanding how the brain functions and how individuals can harness its full potential through scientifically backed memory and learning strategies. His journey from struggling with memory retention to mastering effective learning techniques has shaped his mission to share these insights with others.

Fascinated by the power of neuroplasticity and the latest cognitive technologies, Abhit seeks to bridge the gap between scientific knowledge and practical application. His writing reflects this passion, providing readers with actionable strategies to improve their memory, focus, and overall learning abilities.

Beyond his academic and writing pursuits, Abhit continues to explore how technological advancements can further enhance brain function and learning potential. Through this book, he hopes to inspire readers, whether students or professionals, to unlock their brain's potential and achieve success in their personal and academic endeavors.

Reach out me at tomarabhit9@gmail.com
Instagram: https://www.instagram.com/imtomar09

Acknowledgement

Writing this book has been an incredible journey, and I would not have been able to complete it without the support, feedback, and encouragement of many wonderful people.

First and foremost, I would like to express my deepest gratitude to my **family**. Your unwavering belief in me, your patience, and your constant encouragement have been the foundation on which this book was built. Every word written here is a reflection of the strength and support you have given me. Thank you for standing by me through every challenge and celebrating every achievement.

I am also immensely thankful to **Pinky**, my dear friend from Orissa, for her invaluable insights and excellent feedback throughout the process. Her thoughtful review of the book and encouragement pushed me to refine my work and present it at its best.

A special thank you to **Kapil Sharma**, a talented student from Delhi University who has written over 50 poems. His creativity and poetic perspective helped me see the writing process from a new angle, making the content more engaging and impactful.

I am deeply grateful to **Aslay Raghuvanshi and Deepak kumar**, my childhood friend, who has been by my side through every situation, offering unwavering support. There presence has been a constant source of strength and inspiration throughout this journey.

I also want to thank **Neeraj Kumar Yadav**, a close friend from my master's degree, who provided invaluable support in reviewing the content. His feedback helped sharpen the ideas and ensure clarity in the chapters.

A big thank you to **Deepak Kumar, Sujit Gurjar, Shivam Kumar** for their help in deciding the cover design and suggesting changes. Their creative input was crucial in shaping the visual aspect of the book.

I must also acknowledge **Harshvardhan Singh**, **Raja Parma**r, and **Aslay Raghuvanshi** once again—my three pillars. Their constant support in every step of the way, from brainstorming to finalizing the content, kept me motivated and on track. I couldn't have done it without you.

Finally, to all my friends—thank you for your encouragement, feedback, and for being there when I needed advice or a push to keep going. Each one of you has played a part in the creation of this book, and for that, I am eternally grateful.

Your support has been instrumental in making this book a reality, and I dedicate this work to you all.

With sincere appreciation,
Abhit Tomar

Bibliography

1. Baddeley, Alan D., Eysenck, Michael W., & Anderson, Michael C.
   Memory. 2nd ed. Psychology Press, 2015.
   This book provides a thorough exploration of memory, from how it is formed to how it is retrieved, with practical insights for students and professionals alike.
2. Brown, Peter C., Roediger, Henry L., & McDaniel, Mark A.
   Make It Stick: The Science of Successful Learning. Harvard University Press, 2014.
   A highly recommended book that offers evidence-based learning techniques, including the power of active recall, spaced repetition, and retrieval practice for effective long-term retention.
3. Kahneman, Daniel.
   Thinking, Fast and Slow. Farrar, Straus and Giroux, 2011.
   This bestselling book delves into the two modes of thinking—fast, instinctive thinking and slow, deliberate thinking—offering valuable insights into how memory and cognition work in daily life.
4. Foer, Joshua.
   Moonwalking with Einstein: The Art and Science of Remembering Everything. Penguin Books, 2011.
   Joshua Foer's personal journey of mastering memory techniques, including the memory palace and visualization, serves as a highly readable and inspiring guide to anyone looking to improve their memory skills.
5. Ericsson, Anders, & Pool, Robert.
   Peak: Secrets from the New Science of Expertise. Mariner Books, 2016.
   This book focuses on deliberate practice and how specific techniques, including memory exercises, can be used to develop expertise in any field.
6. Squire, Larry R., & Kandel, Eric R.
   Memory: From Mind to Molecules. 2nd ed. W.H. Freeman, 2008.
   A comprehensive guide to the neuroscience of memory, explaining how our brains form, store, and retrieve memories at a molecular level.
7. Atkinson, Richard C., & Shiffrin, Richard M.
   Human Memory: A Proposed System and its Control Processes. Stanford

University, 1968.
A foundational work in memory theory that introduces the multi-store model of memory, explaining how sensory memory, short-term memory, and long-term memory interact.

8. Tulving, Endel.
Elements of Episodic Memory. Oxford University Press, 1985.
This book explores episodic memory, which involves remembering personal experiences, and how it differs from semantic memory (general knowledge).
9. Mlodinow, Leonard.
Subliminal: How Your Unconscious Mind Rules Your Behavior. Pantheon Books, 2012.
Mlodinow explains how much of our behavior and memory processing happens unconsciously, offering fascinating insights into how memory works behind the scenes.
10. Maguire, Eleanor A., Gadian, David G., Johnsrude, Ingrid S., Good, Chris D., Ashburner, John, Frackowiak, Richard S. J., & Frith, Chris D.
Navigation-related structural change in the hippocampi of taxi drivers. Proceedings of the National Academy of Sciences, 2000.
A key study on neuroplasticity that shows how the hippocampus—the brain's memory center—can change and grow in response to regular use, as seen in London taxi drivers who memorize city maps.
11. Ericsson, K. Anders, & Lehmann, Andreas C.
Expert and Exceptional Performance: Evidence of Maximal Adaptation to Task Constraints. Annual Review of Psychology, 1996.
This review focuses on how experts develop exceptional memory and performance through deliberate practice and task-specific adaptations.
12. Buzan, Tony.
The Mind Map Book: Unlock your Creativity, Boost Your Memory, Change Your Life. BBC Active, 2010.
Tony Buzan's book on mind mapping provides practical strategies for organizing thoughts, improving memory, and enhancing creativity through visual techniques.
13. Levitin, Daniel J.
The Organized Mind: Thinking Straight in the Age of Information Overload. Dutton, 2014.
This book discusses how to manage and organize information in today's world, where we are constantly bombarded with data, and provides

practical strategies for improving focus and memory.

14. Roediger, Henry L., & Butler, Andrew C.
The Critical Role of Retrieval Practice in Long-Term Retention. Trends in Cognitive Sciences, 2011.
This article discusses the importance of retrieval practice, or actively recalling information, as one of the most effective learning strategies for improving long-term memory retention.
15. Tulving, Endel, & Donaldson, Wayne.
Organization of Memory. Academic Press, 1972.
A classic text on how memory is organized, focusing on the cognitive and neural processes that underpin how we structure, store, and retrieve information.
16. Shakuntala Devi.
Figuring: The Joy of Numbers. HarperCollins, 2005.
A book on numbers by the Indian mathematical prodigy Shakuntala Devi, explaining how numbers can be understood and memorized more effectively through play and visualization.
17. Eric Jensen.
Brain-Based Learning: The New Paradigm of Teaching. Corwin Press, 2008.
Jensen explores how the brain learns and retains information, offering brain-based strategies for enhancing memory, focus, and learning.
18. Medina, John.
Brain Rules: 12 Principles for Surviving and Thriving at Work, Home, and School. Pear Press, 2008.
A user-friendly book that explains how understanding how your brain works can improve your memory, productivity, and learning ability.
19. Carnegie, Dale.
How to Win Friends and Influence People. Simon & Schuster, 1936.
While this book is about human relations, Carnegie provides practical tips on remembering names and connecting with people, which aligns with memory techniques for social interactions.
20. Foerde, Karin, Knowlton, Barbara J., & Poldrack, Russell A.
Modulation of Competing Memory Systems by Distraction. Proceedings of the National Academy of Sciences, 2006.
This research explores how multitasking and distractions affect memory, reinforcing the importance of focus for effective learning.

Glossary

Active Recall

A learning technique that involves actively testing your knowledge by trying to retrieve information from memory, rather than passively reviewing notes or textbooks.

Chunking

A memory technique that involves breaking down large amounts of information into smaller, more manageable "chunks" or units, making it easier to remember.

Encoding

The first stage of memory where information is transformed into a form that can be stored in the brain, such as visual, auditory, or semantic encoding.

Flashcards

A study aid that uses cards with questions or prompts on one side and answers on the other, used for active recall and spaced repetition.

Focus

The ability to concentrate on a single task or piece of information is essential for effective learning and memory retention.

Memory Palace

A mnemonic device involves visualizing a familiar place (such as a house or street) and mentally placing information at specific locations within that place, making it easier to recall later.

Mind Map

A visual representation of ideas and concepts arranged around a central theme helps organize information and illustrate relationships between concepts.

Mnemonic

A tool or technique that helps improve memory by linking information to something more memorable, such as rhymes, acronyms, or associations.

Pegging Technique

A memory technique that involves associating numbers or lists with pre-set "pegs" or objects (such as "one = sun"), which helps to recall items in a specific order.

Pomodoro Technique

A time management method that involves breaking work into intervals of focused study (usually 25 minutes) followed by short breaks (usually 5 minutes).

Retrieval Practice

A learning strategy where you practice recalling information from memory to strengthen long-term retention, often through quizzes or self-testing.

Spaced Repetition

A memory technique where information is reviewed at increasing intervals, allowing for better long-term retention by reinforcing the memory before it fades.

Visualization

A memory technique that involves creating vivid mental images to represent information, making it easier to remember and recall abstract concepts.

Working Memory

A cognitive system responsible for temporarily holding information available for processing is often used for tasks like reasoning, learning, and comprehension.

Long-Term Memory

The part of the memory system where information is stored indefinitely, as opposed to short-term memory, which holds information temporarily.

Attention

The cognitive process of selectively concentrating on specific information while ignoring other perceivable information is crucial for the effective encoding of memories.

Neuroplasticity

The brain's ability to reorganize itself by forming new neural connections throughout life, allows the brain to adapt to new learning and experiences.

BDNF (Brain-Derived Neurotrophic Factor)

A protein that supports the growth, maintenance, and survival of neurons, playing a crucial role in brain function and memory formation, often enhanced through physical activity.

www.ingramcontent.com/pod-product-compliance
Lightning Source LLC
LaVergne TN
LVHW041231150826
845673LV00008B/2359

* 9 7 9 8 8 9 5 5 6 7 4 3 2 *